NANTUCKET

IN COLOR

Profiles of America

NANTUCKET

in Color

A Collection of Color
Photographs by

PETER H. DREYER

With an Introductory Text
and Notes on the Illustrations by

EDOUARD A. STACKPOLE

HASTINGS HOUSE · PUBLISHERS

New York, 10016

PUBLISHED 1973 BY HASTINGS HOUSE, PUBLISHERS, INC.
Reprinted May, 1976
Reprinted February, 1979

Published simultaneously in Canada by
Saunders, of Toronto, Ltd., Don Mills, Ontario

Library of Congress Cataloging in Publication Data

Stackpole, Edouard A., *Nantucket in Color*

(Profiles of America)
1. Nantucket, Mass.—Description and travel—Views.
I. Dreyer, Peter H., illus. II. Title.
F72.N2S67   917.44′97′044   73–13916
ISBN 0–8038–5030–1

Printed and bound in Hong Kong by Mandarin Publishers Limited

CONTENTS

Introduction

The island of Nantucket and the town of the same name occupy a unique place in the ranks of America's summer resorts. The home of some 4,000 permanent residents it annually attracts more than six times that number, many of whom are regular summer residents and others visitors who swell the crowds of tourists making day trips. The appeal of Nantucket is legendary, setting it aside from the usual New England seacoast resort. While its invigorating climate, its facilities for modern living, its sailing and swimming opportunities and its open heathland and sandy beaches are in themselves great attractions, the basic quality of its appeal is the historic background of the old town.

Nestled along the inner curve of its harbor, the town is a striking example of an old seafaring place with few visible evidences of the modern scene. Two centuries ago Nantucket was the greatest whaling port in the Colonies, the founder of a new maritime industry known as the Southern Whale Fishery. Just a century ago its once extensive business was gone, and the resultant depression found the town with only a quarter of its once peak population of 8,000. But this economic disaster had a surprising aftermath. No new buildings replaced whaling's activities; attempts to introduce factories were unsuccessful; the old town fell asleep.

Then came a new means of livelihood—the summer business. Gradually, the unique appeal of the place became widespread. The ancient dwellings of the whalemen were restored and preserved and the larger mansions became rooming houses. As the nineteenth century gave way to the twentieth the town emerged as an architectural jewel in its island setting. The sturdy homes and dignified mansions which whale oil built now serve to reflect the ancient glory of a seafaring past and the cobbled Main Street, winding lanes and narrow byways lead into a rich historical saga.

Geologists have taken an especial interest in the origins of Nantucket Island. An old Indian legend describes a giant—a mighty chief—tossing his huge moccasin full of sand out to sea, thus creating the sandy spot. It is true that a giant did create Nantucket, but it was a geological giant—an immense glacier dropping the earth from the edge of its icy shelf to create this island in the sea as a terminal moraine.

There are many fascinating evidences of the "Glacier's gift." Deep below the island's surface is a strata of blue clay, intermingled with pebbles. Above this a layer of gravel and then sand, so that when the rain water seeps down through it is retained by the clay and the island becomes a great natural reservoir of pure water. The marks of the glacier as it scooped the surface bring out the undulating areas, with ponds and valleys and bluff-lined shores. The stretches of white sand beaches, the boulders in Saul's Hills, the shell deposits at Sankaty Head, the inner curves of Coatue's sandy length, and the outwash plains of the southern sections of the main island—all are constant reminders of nature's creative forces.

The shape of the island is that of a crescent, giving it the appearance of a sailor's hammock suspended from its hooks in a whaler's cabin. Great Point to the north and east and Smith's Point to the west are the curved ends of the crescent forming an extensive outer roadstead, with two long jetties extending out in the bay from the north shore. The inner harbor is almost completely land-locked extending from the wharf area and the town on the western side to the east, where only a narrow sand bar forms a barrier between the open Atlantic and the quiet waters of the upper harbor. In this protected inland bay sailing by young and old may be enjoyed, with the open sea always beckoning the more experienced mariners.

The outlying land of the island proper retains its old name of "commons." Here the open heath provides a veritable paradise for nature-lovers, with an astonishing array of wildflowers, thickets of scrub oak, groves of pine, stretches of mealy-plum and bayberry, and green mazes of swamp where wild grape and high bush blueberry grow in profusion. Extensive cranberry bogs provide an industry for island firms. Rutted roads lead meandering routes across the land, best enjoyed by strollers and bicyclists.

Much of the charm of Nantucket's origins is carried along with the retention of the old Indian names—Coskata, Wauwinet, Squam, Polpis, Quaise, Nobadeer, Weeweeder and Madaket—all constant reminders of the first occupants of this "Faraway Island," as the aborigines called it. Geographically removed from the pace of mainland life Nantucket has had environmental protection through an Historic Districts Act, coupled with the invaluable activities of the Conservation Foundation. By preserving the physical evidences of its historic past, Nantucket serves as a unique memorial to her creators, enabling those of the present to recapture the spirit of America's seafarers and to gain a better understanding of the people who did so much to establish our maritime heritage.

Nantucket—Island and Town

by

EDOUARD A. STACKPOLE

I N ITS location well out in the Atlantic, off the southeastern coast of Massachusetts, Nantucket Island has long occupied a unique place in the annals of America. Once the headquarters of American whaling, it is now one of the most sought after resorts in the nation, presenting an unusual atmospheric charm that appeals to all who enjoy residing or vacationing in an island community which offers all the conveniences of modern living in an historical setting.

Possessing the advantages of an equable climate, Nantucket provides opportunities for recreation and pleasant living comparable to any resort in New England. But the island's outstanding asset is its historic town, often described as the best preserved maritime community in this country. What makes this fact especially significant to historians is that it has been truly a town for over two and one-half centuries, rather than a village or hamlet, and remains as an outstanding example of how our ancestors lived and developed a maritime community. First called Sherborn, the town was later designated Nantucket—thus becoming the only combination of town, county and island bearing the same name existing in the nation.

From the standpoint of history this island town possesses a unique position in the story of American life. Described by Daniel Webster early in the nineteenth century as "The unknown city in the ocean," its development as a seaport, its architectural pattern of growth, and its religious and social characteristics combine to create an extraordinary record. So well preserved are its old houses along the streets and lanes that it serves as a visible example of how a seafaring people lived in the eighteenth and nineteenth centuries.

Not so many years ago it was the Old World—Europe—to which America looked in respect to traditional and cultural heritage. Not so today; as a nation we have come of age; we find our roots and inspirations in our own land. And more and more New England has become America's Old World. Here we find the narrative of our beginnings, a compelling epic revealing the struggles, the successes and failures of those who created a great nation. Providing a stirring chapter in the story the annals of Nantucket may be considered a colorful and important part of the narrative, tracing as it does the development of an industry that became an important asset in Colonial days and then became an economic bulwark in the early years of the Republic.

*   *   *

Nantucket's earliest history is a mystery. While the Indians were the first inhabitants, a branch tribe of the Algonquins, there is no clear knowledge of when they first came to the island, and their traditions were never transcribed, unhappily. When Thomas Mayhew, a prosperous merchant of Watertown, Massachusetts, was granted the Island of Martha's Vineyard from the Crown of England he soon after acquired the rights for the neighboring island of Nantucket. From the year 1641, when Mayhew used the "Land Far Off at Sea," as the Indian name for Nantucket indicates, as grazing pastures for his sheep and cattle the island may be said to have first felt the tread of the white man's feet. At this time Mayhew introduced Christianity to the Indians as he had to the aborigines of Martha's Vineyard.

While Bartholomew Gosnold, the English mariner, is said to have been the first to discover Nantucket's low-lying shores, the best claim to actual recording of its presence may be that of Captain George Weymouth who, on May 13, 1605, finding his ship amidst the shoals in latitude 41 degrees north, sent a man to masthead who sighted "a white, sandy cliff" then some 12 miles distant. Soundings were taken and they made for the land but the frothing appearance of the rips between forced them off and they never landed.

It was this same expanse of Nantucket shoals which played a key role in history several years later. It will be recalled that the *Mayflower*, having crossed the Atlantic and making a landfall at Cape Cod, then "resolved to stand to ye southward (ye wind and weather being faire) to find some place about Hudson's River for their habitation." But after sailing half a day the *Mayflower* found herself "amongst dangerous shoals and roaring breakers, and . . . they conceived themselves in great danger . . . and resolved to bear up again for the Cape, and thought themselves happy to get out of those dangers before night overtook them . . . and the next day they got into ye Cape harbor. . . ."

Thus it was that Nantucket's shoals were an all important factor in changing both the course of the *Mayflower* and history, as the Pilgrim fathers decided to land at a place called Plymouth on their crude chart and an American epoch began.

Having obtained from the Nantucket Indians his first deed after acquiring the Royal rights to the island, Thomas Mayhew was approached by a group of Englishmen who had settled around Newbury and Salisbury in the Massachusetts Bay Colony and who wanted to settle elsewhere, away from the Puritan domination in both religious and social life. Mayhew knew these men, and sold them his rights to Nantucket for "Thirty Pounds in good Merchantable Pay and Two Beaver Hats, one for myself and one for my wife." Nine men became partners in the purchase—Tristram Coffin, Thomas Macy, Christopher Hussey, Richard Swain, Thomas Barnard, Peter Coffin, Stephen Greenleaf, John Swain and William Pike—with Mayhew himself retaining a one-twentieth part of "all lands and privileges." The deed was dated July 2, 1659.

The first purchasers agreed that each was to be allowed to choose a partner who should join in the venture on equal terms, and those so chosen were Nathaniel and Edward Starbuck, Tristram Coffin, Jr., Thomas Look, James Coffin, John Smith, Robert Barnard, Robert Pike and Thomas Coleman. Thus was created the "Proprietors of The Common and Undivided Lands of Nantucket," an organization which still exists. Later, there were fourteen half-shares—or seven whole shares—granted additional settlers. Under this system all land acquired on Nantucket, except the original house-lots and the Quaise holdings of Mayhew, carried one twenty-seventh ownership for each share holder.

First actual settlement on the island by the whites took place in the fall of 1659, when Thomas Macy and his wife Sarah and their four children, accompanied by Edward Starbuck and Isaac Coleman, then a young boy, erected a rough habitation near the landing place at the west end or Madaket part of the island and there spent the first winter. The following year they were joined by Tristram Coffin and the other partners, and the homesteads were laid out along the chain of ponds stretching across the western center of the island.

Thus Nantucket's first white settlers came along the highway of the sea to a remote part of New England which they had deliberately chosen as their future homes. They came in search of freedom, where their everyday lives would not be dominated by the stern rule of the Puritans of Massachusetts Bay. Through this one significant fact these people revealed both courage and determination, traits of character having much to do with their founding of not just another settlement but a unique colony which was to develop into a virtually independent maritime kingdom.

Recognizing the need for skilled artisans the first company of the

Nantucketers invited as "half-share" partners men versed in trades—surveyors, carpenters, millers and cobblers—as well as experienced fishermen, among the latter being Edward Cartwright and Captain John Gardner. As might have been expected there was soon an effort by the "half-share" men to gain an equal representation in the affairs of the settlement, and among the dissenters was Peter Foulger, the future grandfather of Benjamin Franklin. But before this transpired other political factors had affected the island's history.

While the first settlers were laying out their homesteads England was engaged in Civil War and New Amsterdam had been recaptured by the Dutch, a factor in the embryo settlement's life as New York Colony was the governing parent. The attitude of the New Englanders towards the armies of Cromwell and the Royalists in the mother country was similar to that of the brow-beaten wife whose husband was engaged in a mortal combat with a bear. Torn between wifely loyalty and a natural resentment for her husband's cruelty towards her, she kept muttering: "Go it husband—go it bear!"

When Charles II found himself on the restored throne of England in 1664, he made a new grant to his brother, the Duke of York, of a large part of the lands first set aside to the Earl of Stirling by his father. This transaction included Nantucket. A new Governor, Francis Lovelace, was appointed for New York Colony and in May 1670, he ordered all claimants to lands on the island to appear before him within four months to prove their titles. However it was not until a year had passed that Tristram Coffin and Thomas Macy went to New York as representatives of the proprietors. A new patent was issued to them and their associates, the consideration being an annual payment of "four barrels of merchantable codfish" and that the land purchased from the Indians have their titles ratified by the Royal Governor.

It was at this time that the settlement on Nantucket was incorporated and in 1673 Governor Lovelace gave it the name of Sherborn, by which it was known down to 1795.

One of the "half-share" men, Captain John Gardner, now came to the fore through his appointment by Lovelace as the "Captain of the Foot Company." Up to this time Tristram Coffin was the leading figure politically, aided by his five sons and two sons-in-law, among the latter being Nathaniel Starbuck. A strong force, Coffin wanted to continue the settlement as a place where the land custom of England would be a continuing and prevailing condition. To bring matters to a head, the appointment of Richard Gardner, brother of Captain John, to be the Chief Magistrate of Nantucket became a political factor in the struggle in the offing.

Captain John Gardner not only represented the "half-share" men but also advanced the idea of a true democracy on the island. He found in Peter

Foulger a strong supporter, along with other of the "half-share" group, but he was also ably seconded by Thomas Macy and others of the "Old Guard." While the Dutch momentarily held New York (July 1673 to October 1674) both of the island factions marked time; but when the English re-took New York and Governor Thomas Andros replaced Lovelace the Nantucket "insurrection" was renewed in earnest. Soon the new Royal Governor was bombarded with petitions and counter-petitions by the two factions. On the Vineyard Mayhew sided with the Coffins.

At first the Coffin party gained an ascendancy when Thomas Macy decided to re-join the conservatives. It was at this time that Peter Foulger was found guilty of contempt of His Majesty's authority and was placed in a crude jail for several months. The record book of the court sessions, which Peter refused to produce when he was dismissed from his duties as clerk, was at this time lost and never found. More than two long years of controversy evolved before Governor Andros took sides and restored the Gardner faction to power. By 1680 the revolt of the "half-share" men was completely successful with the appointment of Captain John Gardner as Chief Magistrate.

Peter Foulger had been an important man in the early years as not only a surveyor and miller but an interpreter for the Indians. His influence was never more greatly apparent than at the time the famous Indian chief King Philip came to Nantucket and tried to enlist the aid of the local tribes for his planned insurrection. He returned to the mainland disillusioned. Peter Foulger's counsel was accepted instead of Philip's fiery oratory.

The victory of the democratic society in Nantucket was one which had a marked effect. It demonstrated the ability of the islanders to determine their own destiny peacefully; it also revealed the strong personalities of the founding fathers. It was the first of three powerful influences which were to set the course for Nantucket's future.

Tristram Coffin died in 1681. A few years later his grandson, Jethro Coffin, married Captain John Gardner's daughter Mary thus uniting two once-warring factions. The house which the young couple had built for them in 1686 still stands on Sunset Hill, now open to the public as one of the possessions of the Nantucket Historical Association. It is a monument to the end of one stirring period in the island's history and the beginning of another.

In 1681, the Duke of York ascended the English throne as King James II and he appointed Thomas Dongan as the new Governor of New York Colony. Dongan issued a new Patent for Nantucket in 1687 and this is considered as the actual starting point for all the island's land title lay-outs. The Dongan Patent is preserved to this day at the Registry of Deeds office at the new Town Building on Broad Street. By an Act of Parliament, passed in 1692, all the islands Mayhew secured from Royal authority in 1641 were transferred from

New York Colony to the Province of Massachusetts Bay, and Nantucket was included.

*   *   *

The second of the powerful influences that were to shape the rural settlement of the island was religious—the coming of Quakerism. For three decades there had been no established church on the island and some of the traveling members of the Society of Friends visiting here sought to introduce this religion among the inhabitants. In this effort they were able to secure the support of Mary Coffin Starbuck, the wife of Nathaniel Starbuck, and a leader in the community; and in the large room of the Starbuck dwelling, overlooking Hummock Pond, the first meetings were held. The house now removed in part into the present town is known as Parliament House, as it was also used in the early gatherings of the men who served as the officials in the local government. Within a decade the first of the Quaker Meeting Houses was erected and within the early years of the eighteenth century the Quakers became the dominant feature of Nantucket life, controlling not only the religious life of the island but the social and economic life as well.

The first of the Nantucket Meetings of the Society of Friends was formed in 1704, and the first meeting house was built in 1711. Formed in this same year was a branch of the Congregational Church. The rapid growth of Quakerism demonstrated more vividly than words the acceptance of this philosophy of religion and life by the inhabitants. For over a century and a quarter the Society of Friends on Nantucket was not only the dominant force in the religious life of the community but in the social and economic affairs, as well. No other place in America was so controlled and in no other community in the new world was such a large proportion of the inhabitants members of this faith.

*   *   *

The third of the great influences which shaped the island's destiny was whaling. It was a calling which became an industry and a tradition in one, virtually creating a kingdom in the sea and establishing a new economic force in Colonial America.

In the study of Nantucket's whaling it is important to recognize that the islanders were not the first Colonial whalers. The people of Plymouth Colony, the residents along the shores of Cape Cod, the settlers at the east end of Long Island were cutting up drift whales and were capturing whales along-shore while the Nantucketers were busy settling their homes. What marked the introduction of Nantucket into whaling was similar to these other localities— selling whale oil in the shire towns of Boston and New York.

The difference was in the location of Nantucket, like a mother ship in the ocean closer to the migratory routes of the whales. The islanders not only took the whales along-shore but went out to sea looking for them. Thus they developed a new Colonial industry—deep sea whaling. Soon their sloops were spending weeks well out at sea seeking and capturing right whales. And then, on one historic day in the late 1690s, one of the sloop masters sighted a whale whose spouting revealed he was of a different species. Pursuing and taking him, the master found that they had killed a spermaceti whale, whose oil was far more valuable than any other of these ocean mammals. From that day until the last whaleship sailed from the island the Nantucketer specialized in the pursuit of the sperm whale.

With the development of the new industry came the necessity of utilizing the island's only large anchorage area—the Great Harbor, as it was called. The full use of this natural waterfront meant wharves and warehouses. As a result a town was laid out and built here rising virtually from the water's edge and ascending the gently rising slopes of the Wesco Hills. Carefully did the Proprietors divide the land into house lot sections—Wesco, the Fish Lots, West Monomoy. Each inhabitant was given his proportionate part.

The old farming locality of Sherborn soon found many of its dwellings moved to the new settlement. The town grew rapidly from 1680 to 1725. Lanes which led from the original settlement to the new became highways— North Street, Centre Street, State Street, Duke Street—names now retained among the principal streets of the town. The original house lot sections were expanded with interlacing lanes weaving the town into a pattern it still retains and providing the closely knit pattern which has become its outstanding characteristic.

The first of the four permanent wharves, Straight Wharf, was built in 1723 by the Macys. This marked the decade when the islanders began selling their oil directly to London thus avoiding the middleman of the Boston merchant. Soon other wharves appeared, Old South in 1740; Old North in 1750; New North in 1770, and Commercial Wharf in 1790. Warehouses, sail lofts, cooper shops, ship chandleries and shipsmith shops became conspicuous parts of the waterfront, with oil refineries, candle houses and rope walks being erected in the town and adjacent fields.

It has always been a matter for astonishment to historians that the Nantucket mariners of the eighteenth century could have created such a whaling port that would become the very center of Colonial whaling. As an enterprise it was truly a community effort involving not only the vessels making the voyages but the several trades ashore necessary for fitting them out. A significant factor in this relationship of sea and land was the social fabric of the community, as after the second generation there was considerable intermarriage among the island families and loyalties were strongly evident.

Adoption of the philosophy of the Society of Friends strengthened this family association. The men who made the casks for the whale oil, who fitted the rigging, cut the spars and sewed the sails of the ship were sons, brothers, cousins and neighbors of the men who sailed the vessels and rowed off in the whaleboat in pursuit of the whale.

Whale oil and sperm candles were Nantucket's exports in a world market including the West Indies, England, France, Holland, Spain and even the Baltic. With the advent of the American Revolution the island had reached its first peak of prosperity with a fleet of 85 whaleships, as many sloops or packets to carry oil to market and bring home supplies, a population of nearly 7,000 of which one quarter was seamen. Her ships had become the pioneers in a new industry called the Southern Whale Fishery and were as familiar with the South Atlantic and the Falkland Islands as they were with the Davis Straits to the north.

The Revolution was one of the most disastrous periods in the island's history. In a society dominated by the Quakers Nantucket, virtually an independent maritime community, adopted a role of neutrality. Between the devil and the deep the leaders managed to maintain this position, but at a terrible cost. The whaling fleet was decimated, the population dwindled, business came to a standstill and the once prosperous town was close to ruin. The aftermath of the war at first only increased the scope of the economic misfortunes as groups of whaling families migrated to Nova Scotia, New York State and even to England and France. In the latter cases they had been invited to take out whaleships from London and Dunkirk, so that a situation developed where Nantucket as the originator of the Southern Whale Fishery found competition from European ships manned by fellow-islanders.

But the traditional enterprise of the old home port came to the fore. Even before the Treaty of Paris had officially ended the war, the ship *Bedford*, under Captain William Mooers, sailed from Nantucket to London loaded with whale oil and, early in February 1783, hoisted the first American flag ever displayed in a British port when she anchored under the very shadow of the Tower of London. But recovery was slow as the chief market for oil, England, closed her doors with a high duty. The decade from 1785 to 1795 was crucial but the sturdy islanders, following the pattern of their closely knit industry, gradually restored the whaling supremacy. By 1793 the fleet numbered 30 vessels, now ranging around Cape Horn to the distant Pacific; there were 577 houses, 5,000 inhabitants, two-thirds of whom were Quakers; and among new industries was a sail-making manufactury.

From the advent of the nineteenth century the whaling prosperity of Nantucket grew steadily. There were set-backs—the Quasi-War with France, the war of 1812, which found the fleet in the far-off Pacific and then forced

22

to run the blockade of the Royal Navy; competition from the swiftly rising port of New Bedford, as well as New London and Sag Harbor. When Josiah Freeman visited in the early 1800s he found a town of 7,000 people, with 850 dwellings, 63 stores, a large number of shops, besides candle houses, rope walks, etc., 5 windmills, 2 Quaker Meeting Houses, 1 Congregational and 1 Methodist, 2 banks, 2 insurance offices, a Free Masons Hall and over 100 ships.

The second peak of whaling prosperity came in 1845 when new architectural designs made their appearance among the traditional styles of the earlier period. Many a stirring page had now been written by the island whalemen. Their pioneering instinct had led the American and European counterparts into the Indian, Pacific and Arctic Oceans; more than two score of islands in the South Seas had been discovered by the exploring mariners and as many more re-charted. The names of the Pacific Bank and Pacific Club on Main Street's Square are reminders of this epoch in our whaling history.

Always a decided handicap to the industry was a series of sand bars stretching across the outer entrance to the harbor, known as Nantucket Bar. This made it necessary to lighten the ships outside, increasing expenses in outfitting as well as discharging cargo of ships newly arrived. An ingenious floating dry-dock called "The Camels," had been invented, lasting well into the 1840s, but it came too late to check the decline of island whaling. It had always been ironic that the present stone jetties that cut a channel through Nantucket Bar were erected in 1881–1889, some half century too late!

It took a series of disasters to bring Nantucket's whaling to a swift end. First came the Great Fire of 1846, a major conflagration which totally destroyed the entire waterfront, wharves, warehouses, etc., and burned out the main business section. The re-building process was remarkable but the downward trend had already set in. Then came the migration of some 400 islanders in the Gold Rush period to California. The Civil War found nearly 500 men entering both Army and Navy (Nantucket was the banner town of the Commonwealth of Massachusetts), and engaging in work off-island. Competing ports attracted local whalemen. The fleet here dwindled so that by 1869, when the bark *Oak* sailed, the glorious chapter of Nantucket Whaling had ended.

Depression settled over the town like a cloud. Grass grew through the cobbles of once bustling streets, houses remained unpainted, fences in disrepair, house-top walks were removed, even some of the dwellings were sold and taken down for removal to the mainland. The town became a ghostly place, the wharves empty but for a few sloops and schooners, an air of melancholy pervading. Some merchants attempted to start new industries—a fishing fleet, shoe factory, linen manufactury—but all in turn failed. The population had dwindled to 2,120 by 1870.

*   *   *

Then came the first stirrings of a new activity—summer business. Nantucket was being discovered as an excellent place to spend a summer vacation. With the 1870s the town gradually emerged as a seasonal resort. Some of the large mansions were converted into boarding houses (one already converted into a hotel) and some of the visitors began erecting summer cottages on the Cliff and along Brant Point. New grocery stores, livery stables and a catboat fleet for fishing enthusiasts marked the transition. The need for providing adequate transportation for this new business brought about a new steamboat line and a slogan, "two boats a day," became a reality, reflecting the growing popularity of the island both as a vacation and a health resort.

  The latent spirit of enterprise so characteristic of Nantucket was revived. To foster this new business it was realized that the natural attractions of the island could be enhanced by modern innovations tending to make them even more inviting. First came the introduction of a "city" water supply, and pipes were laid from the spring-fed Wannacomet Pond in 1881. Gas manufactured here for lighting had already been introduced and electric lights became a feature in 1889. Three new hotels were opened in a decade. A narrow-gauge steam railroad was built in 1881 and extended to 'Sconset four years later. The government laid a telegraph cable in 1881 and a Weather Bureau station was established. The telephone became a reality by 1891 and before the advent of the twentieth century one of the most important modern improvements of all was installed in the town, a sewage disposal system. Only one of the innovations of the new century was rejected, and this by official vote, the introduction of the automobile. This ban was continued until the spring of 1918 when, by the narrow margin of only 40 votes, the long argued ban was lifted, to the regret of many.

*   *   *

As a rare and valuable combination of a town preserving both eighteenth- and nineteenth-century atmosphere. Nantucket provides both architects and historians an unusual opportunity to study the visible evidences of the past. The early settlers built their homes in the style of their English homeland, simple, sturdy structures with a long-sloping roof to the rear, known as the "lean-to" design, of which the Oldest House, erected in 1686, is an excellent example.

  With the growth of the community the dwellings erected in the eighteenth century reflect the stalwart character of the inhabitants of Sherborn. Such

24

houses as those of Elihu Coleman on Hawthorn Lane, the Josiah Coffin homestead on North Liberty Street, the Richard Gardner house on West Chester and Shubael Gardner on Main Street are excellent examples of their times. When the two-storey front and rear types came into general use by 1750 the houses retained their simple lines, built to the tradition of the Quaker community, compact and with the ship-builders' recognition of the utilization of every inch of available space.

The next architectural period came with the post-Revolution, the Federalist style, strongly built and larger but still bearing the stamp of the Quaker influence. With the coming of the wave of whaling prosperity in the 1830–1850 eras, the Greek Revival style caught favor and several imposing mansions were built on Main Street, vying with the brick Georgian-style houses erected in the 1830–1840 period. This break with the traditional types not only reflected the growing wealth of the whale oil merchants but the waning influence of the Society of Friends within the community. The ranks of the Quakers had been split by the emergence of divergent forces within the Society—the Gurneyites, followers of Joseph Gurney, and others. In these times the other religious organizations had grown—Congregationalists, Methodists, Unitarians and Baptists—each with new, large meeting houses.

In an odd sequence the decline in the power of the Quakers came with the growth of a new vitality in the social life of the island; and with the architectural changes came the challenge of economic competition. The first inklings of whaling decline were felt while many progressive features were being introduced. It was a paradox but the re-building of the burnt areas after the Great Fire of 1846 was accomplished with a burst of optimism. Some of the fine structures rising from the ashes of the fire were the Atheneum, the Sanford and Easton mansions, and several smaller dwellings, as well as the brick business blocks on Main Street Square.

The deep depression which followed whaling's collapse came at a time when the nation as a whole was experiencing a surge of new building. Thus Nantucket could not afford to tear down old structures for new and as a result the old dwellings were preserved. The period of arrested development was an architectural blessing in disguise. When the time arrived that the charm of the old lines and sturdy construction were becoming more fully appreciated there was a re-awakening of the need to preserve and a number of the ancient houses were restored.

Today the town is a unique example of how preservation and modern living may go hand-in-hand. Nantucket is the only community which may claim to exist in an architectural sense as it did a century and a quarter ago. But it is not a "museum town," it is a living community.

As the summer resort business became the stable economy the newly developed areas on the Cliff and along Brant Point reflected the architectural styles of the 1880s and '90s, with cottages and hotels. And yet even in these areas there are examples of buildings influenced by the older designs. A few of the Victorian-style houses were erected in the town at this time and these are now just past or approaching the century old age.

That the historic past of Nantucket is a living force in the present is the outstanding feature of island life and the architecture of the town is a dramatic evidence of the fact. Here are the homes of mariners who made history, the dwellings of the shipowners, the artisans and the workers who created a veritable kingdom in the sea. Many of these people, both men and women, not only played important roles in island history but left their impress on the nation's story. These islanders shared in a common destiny, an immortality best expressed by the phrase: "This is my own, my native land." America as well as Nantucket is favored by the preservation of this seafaring community.

In 1956, through an act of the Legislature, the town received a welcomed protection through the "Historic Districts Act." A decade later further legislation was passed that included the entire island. Recent events, however, have found the threat of developers posing a situation of grave concern as regards the outlying sections. Whether expected changes may be adapted to the old traditions in a realistic manner is the question for the future.

* * *

At the eastern shores of Nantucket there are several hamlets which have become popular over the years as summer places—Wauwinet, Squam, Quidnet and Siasconset. The latter is the largest and always called 'Sconset, a sizable community with its own water supply, telephone system and all modern conveniences. Originally a collection of huts occupied by the island fishermen during the seasons when the fish were running, the little village was first adopted as the "summer place" for residents of the town. With the growing popularity of the island as a resort, 'Sconset soon attracted its own devotees and in the 1890s it became a favored vacation spot for many of the theatrical folk from New York and became known as the "Actors' Colony."

With the advent of the twentieth century 'Sconset blossomed as a full-fledged summer resort. Most of the old fishermen's huts were refurbished and a number of replicas built in 1881–1883 by an enterprising visitor named Underhill have long since been regarded as "originals." Large summer homes were built on the bluffs overlooking the Atlantic so that today they stretch all the way to the red-banded lighthouse at Sankaty Head.

The preserved huts of the fishermen present an unusual center for the village and many of them go back to the eighteenth century. Tiny, almost miniature dwellings, they never fail to excite the visitor. Just below the high

26

bluff is Codfish Park, once the area where the fishermen hauled up their dories and laid out their wooden platforms for drying fish, but today the location of a number of cottages.

On the South Shore the hamlet of Surfside has its own summer colony clustered around what at one time was the first life saving station built on the island, now a youth hostel. At the west end of the island the village of Madaket has developed steadily in the last quarter century. For years a collection of fishing huts and a life saving station featured this section. Today a considerable number of summer and year-'round dwellings compose an attractive village. In more recent times a real estate development has sprung up close by, raising the inevitable question as to the architectural conformity with traditional designs.

*   *   *

There are several attractive and interesting museums and exhibits which present Nantucket's historical background to the visitor. The Nantucket Historical Association, formed in 1894, has several valuable exhibits, foremost of which is the Whaling Museum located on Broad Street at the head of Steamboat Wharf. Here in a brick structure which once was a sperm candle manufactury is displayed a fascinating collection of whaling implements, a whaleboat, a whale's skeleton, scrimshaw (the folk art of the American whaleman), classic whaling prints and ship masters' portraits and whaleship models. Next door is the Peter Foulger Museum with exhibits covering the history of the island, including such relics as the last surviving hand-pumper fire engine, a carved paddle-box decoration from a side-wheel steamboat, displays of Chinese porcelain, silver, Liverpool pitchers, Staffordshire china, island-made furniture, lightship baskets and paintings by such famous artists as Eastman Johnson. Of more than insular appeal is the tall "Grandfather's" clock and early telescope (1809) made by the Nantucket genius Walter Folger, whose portrait shows a marked resemblance to his cousin, Benjamin Franklin.

Other of the Historical Association's interesting exhibits include the Oldest House, built in 1686; the Old Mill, erected 1746; the Christian (Macy) House (1741); the Old Jail, built in 1805; the Fair Street Rooms, with adjacent Friends Meeting House (1838); the 1800 House, on Mill Street; the little Fire House on Gardner Street and the Hadwen-Satler House, the beautifully restored Greek Revival style mansion on Main Street.

The Nantucket Life Saving Museum, opened in 1972, is the newest of the private museums and is located on the Polpis Road, a carefully built replica of the first life saving station erected on the island in 1874. It features handsomely restored surf-boats, original quarterboards from vessels wrecked on the shoals and shores of the island and an extensive collection of relics and pictures depicting the colorful history of the Humane Society Houses, Life Saving Stations and Coast Guard installations as they relate to Nantucket.

Throughout the town there are other historic structures well worth. visiting. The Kenneth Taylor Gallery on Straight Wharf, now a center for artists, was originally the headquarters of a whaling firm. Next door, the Straight Wharf Theatre was formerly an old sail loft. The waterfront area has gone through a major change in recent years, but close at hand are structures reflecting the early days, such as the American Legion's brick headquarters on Washington Street, once the warehouse for Gorhan Coffin; the Field Brass Foundry, situated at the head of Commercial Wharf; and the Old Town Building, standing between Washington and Union Streets near Main where, until a few years ago, the official offices of the town were incorporated. The restored old office of the Collector of Taxes is open to the public and well worth a visit.

At the foot of Main Street's Square stands the brick Pacific Club, originally the Counting House of William Rotch, one of the most remarkable Colonial merchants in American history. From this building, in 1773, sailed the *Dartmouth* and *Beaver*, bound for London with Nantucket whale oil and which returned with tea to Boston to participate in the famous Boston Tea Party. Also from this structure cleared the ship *Bedford* in 1783, to sail for London where Captain Mooers displayed the first flag of the new United States ever flown in a British port. For over a century the U.S. Custom House, a marine insurance office and headquarters of a shipmasters' group called the Pacific Club, this ancient structure is now owned by the successors of the club.

To the visitor the island and town offer many forms of relaxation— swimming, bicycling, walking, golf, horse-back riding, tennis, sailing, or just enjoying the atmosphere of the historic town. There is a remarkable number of rooming houses where accommodations may be obtained for a week or a month. Many of these are old dwellings, tastefully restored, with all modern conveniences and the hospitality of host or hostess is of the highest order. Modern hotels and inns are also situated in various parts of the town.

Last, but hardly least of the opportunities for pleasure, the vacationist may find strolling through the streets and lanes of the old town an unusual experience, with walks or bicycle trips to the outlying areas providing enjoyment as well. In all cases the clear air, unusual surroundings and restful atmosphere of Nantucket (especially in the off-season months) may bring a stimulation to both mind and body of the perceptive visitor.

The problem of the present-day islander, the resident and the voter is to protect what he has inherited—a unique island and town, a precious segment of the New England and American past. How the challenge is faced will determine the survival or the loss of a fascinating community into whose legacy is woven the history, economy and social life of one of the most interesting chronicles of our American story.

THE PLATES

BRANT POINT LIGHT AT DUSK

Guarding the entrance to Nantucket harbor, Brant Point Lighthouse stands at the very end of the sandy point, protected by rip-rap stone. Placed here in the early years of the present century the small wooden structure is the successor to a long line of light towers that occupied positions close by. Brant Point was the location of the second lighthouse ever erected along the coast of Colonial (British) America, the structure having been built in 1746 at a position several hundred feet inland from the present lighthouse.

A red light illumes the modern lens, and just beyond may be seen the range light, with the tower of the U.S. Coast Guard Station rising on a line further along. Cottages now occupy the site of a busy shipyard of more than a century ago. All vessels entering the commodious harbor come along the shipping channel from the jetties and round Brant Point – the passenger steamers and excursion boats, the cruisers and yachts and sports fishermen, and the numerous smaller craft. Vacationists find the Lighthouse rocks provide an excellent vantage point for viewing the scene.

When large coastal schooners, notably the *Shenandoah*, come into port something of the vanished glory of the days of sail returns, and one is reminded of those stirring times when Nantucket whaleships, home after an absence of years, swept majestically down the channel and came around Brant Point, bringing their oil treasures safely to the old home port.

32

WATERFRONT COTTAGES ALONG OLD WHARVES

In recent years three of the five old wharves have undergone a major change. Straight Wharf, Old South and Commercial wharves are now the location of boat basins, equipped with the services that the modern yachtsman expects, and where fishing shanties and coal sheds once dominated the scene there are now cottages for summer living, shops and artists' studios. The construction of the pilings, cap-logs and retaining planking has altered the scene still further. With the passage of years the elements will bring a gradual shading of the new structures. In the interim the busy atmosphere of the modern world swirls around the waterfront, reminding that Nantucket's livelihood is vitally concerned with the seasonal trade and the services and installations here provide a necessary ingredient towards the business.

Spending a summer month in one of these cottages, virtually living over the waterfront, provides an experience both unique and appealing to many people. The prospect of the wharves is constantly changing, and the tidal flow brings about a sense of the elemental forces. The scene is in the nature of a transition from the modern world to the old town where the flavor of the past brings a blending both felt and seen.

34

THE TOWN NORTHEAST FROM THE STEEPLE

From the vantage point of the North Church (Congregationalist) tower, looking northeast, an excellent view of the town may be enjoyed. In the foreground some of the older dwellings may be seen, with roof-top walks and cupolas and sturdy lines. Centre Street curves away to the left, leading to the area known as "the Cliff," while in the background the cottages and summer homes of the Brant Point section stretch along Beachside. It was nearly a century ago that the first homes made their appearance on Brant Point and the Cliff. Nantucket had been "discovered" as an ideal spot for summer vacations and families from the mainland began establishing residences here. The descendants of many of these families still own and maintain these places, becoming as much a part of island life as the townsfolk whose ancestors were among the early settlers.

36

OLD DESIGNS FOR MODERN LIVING

The architectural designs of the ancient dwellings of Nantucket lend them-selves admirably to modern living. A decade ago a young family decided to build a home "out of town," following the style of the first settlers' homes known as "lean-tos." The result was a structure sturdy and enduring, with a center chimney, two-storey front and long, sloping roof to the rear, and plenty of windows. A split-rail fence served to set off the house, providing a picture that resembles a vista of two centuries ago. The new occupants of the dwelling now enjoy a fully equipped modern home within the framework of the older day.

SCRIMSHAW, FOLK ART OF THE WHALEMEN

The American whalemen have left a heritage of adventure that never fails to excite the interest of both layman and historian. But, along with logbook and journal, they bequeathed an art form—the incising and etching on whale bone and sperm whale ivory known as *scrimshaw*. This is actually a folk art which the whalemen created and practiced during the long hours of their ship-board life. A remarkable variety of these items was produced, along with work boxes inlaid with bone and ivory, crimping wheels for decorative designs on pie crusts, swifts for winding yarn, and knitting needles.

In the shop of Morgan Levine on Straight Wharf a skilled craftsman in the art of scrimshaw plies his trade, His name is Robert Spring, and his artistic creations have given him an enviable and deserved reputation as a craftsman. Working on a sperm whale's ivory tooth, he is shown here creating a design in the old-style tradition.

THE DOME OF THE MARIA MITCHELL OBSERVATORY

This unusual view of the dome on the Maria Mitchell Observatory was taken from the attic window of the house next door where Maria Mitchell was born in 1818. The daughter of William Mitchell, a teacher, mathematician, astronomer and bank cashier, Maria often assisted her father in his work of "rating" chronometers for shipmasters and making observations of the stars with his telescope. On an October night in 1849, while observing the heavens from her father's small observatory on the roof of the Pacific Bank, Miss Mitchell discovered a comet. She reported her find to her father, who notified the outside world of astronomers. It was months later that it became known that Maria Mitchell had made the first discovery of this new comet. Among honors showered on this daughter of Nantucket was a gold medal from the King of Denmark. A decade later she was appointed as the first professor of astronomy at Vassar College in Poughkeepsie, New York.

Early in this century descendants of the Mitchell family, the Hinchmans of Philadelphia, founded the Maria Mitchell Association in her birthplace on Vestal Street. A brick observatory with a bronze dome was erected next door and in 1912 the first Director for the Observatory, Miss Margaret Harwood, arrived on Nantucket to become one of the outstanding and best-beloved personages in the town during the next half century. She retired after four decades of service to that association.

Today, the Maria Mitchell Association maintains the Observatory, the Mitchell homestead, a Library, a Natural Science headquarters at the Hinchman House and the Loines Observatory on Milk Street.

42

FRIENDS BURIAL GROUND, UPPER MAIN STREET

The eighteenth century was still young when the Nantucket Meeting of the Society of Friends built a Meeting House facing Quaker Road at the corner of Upper Main Street. The burial ground surrounded the structure and continued to be used long after a new Meeting House had been built in the town's center. In the tradition of the Society no headstones were used for over 150 years. It was only during the final decades of the Society's presence on the island that a few gravestone markers were permitted and these are located at the north-eastern portion of the ground.

In the dusk of a snowy day, with the old roof lines of the houses in the background, the scene brings back some of the starkness of this island world in the early settlement. Forced to depend upon themselves for survival, remote from any mainland community, the pioneers created their virtual kingdom in the sea. Within that first century they adopted the religious philosophy of the Society of Friends, and the influence of the Quakers had a vital part in shaping the destiny of this island town.

44

A WHARF VISTA OF THE PRESENT

The stroller down Straight Wharf may find the views on either hand of more than passing interest. In the foreground a large barge, moored in Still Dock, acts as a floating warehouse for many lobster pots. These wooden traps for the succulent crustacean are taken fifty to sixty miles off the island's eastern shores where they are dropped to the ocean floor, marked by their buoy moorings and hauled at proper intervals.

The middle view is of the cottages perched on their stilt-like piers on the end of Old North Wharf. In the background may be seen the buildings on Steamboat Wharf, landing place for the Steamship Authority vessels, and a hive of activity during those several times in the day when the boats arrive and depart. Although the changes at this wharf have been many over the years, the exciting scenes of arrivals and departures, the unloading and loading, and the swirl of people moving about continue to be an important part of the island's daily life.

NORTH CHURCH STEEPLE RISES OVER GRAY GABLES

The slender steeple atop the tower of the North Church stands high above the surrounding houses, a symbol of the Christian faith that has so characterized the New England scene in the nineteenth century. The North or Congregational Church on Nantucket goes well back to the early years of the 1720s, and its first meeting house, now the Old North Vestry, still playing an active role in church life, stands at the rear of the larger edifice, proudly showing its more than two centuries of age.

Erected in 1834, the Congregational Meeting House originally had a steeple, and the first bell in the tower was the one originally used for sounding the fifty-two strokes at 7 a.m., 12 noon and 9 p.m. each day, a custom now transferred to the sweet-toned Portuguese bell in the South (Unitarian) Church tower on Orange Street.

Within a few years after its construction the steeple of the North Church was removed because it was believed unsafe and a square tower crowned with minarets replaced it. During the 1930s a young minister accepted the call to the Church, the Rev. Fred D. Bennett, and among his aspirations was to some day restore the steeple. The advent of World War II found him joining the armed services as a Chaplain and he became a career man in the U.S. Navy. Upon his retirement he returned to Nantucket, resumed his pastorate at Old North, and almost immediately began a campaign to restore the steeple. In 1968 his dream came true and the slender white steeple once more became an outstanding feature of the town's skyline. However the actual placement of the steeple in its position on the tower was accomplished in a manner even beyond his original dream—it was literally dropped into place by a helicopter!

48

THE OLD MILL IN WINTER

Standing starkly against a winter sky, with the arms bare of their lattice vanes, the Old Mill is a sentinel amidst its snowy surround. Built in 1746 this mill is the only survivor of four that once stood along the range of hills west of the town. The long, mast-like pole has a heavy wheel at its lower end, so that a team of horses can turn the entire top assembly of the mill around so as to face the prevailing wind.

Visitors to this old structure are amazed at the simplicity of its grinding mechanism. When the vanes catch the wind they turn a 12-by-12 inch main shaft to which is fastened a large wooden wheel under the mill top. A number of wooden teeth, made of hickory, are set in the wheel's perimeter, and these engage an oaken spindle affixed to the top or grinding stone. The corn kernels are poured down the center hole of the top stone and are ground between the moving top stone and the stationary bottom stone. The grain moves along grooves in the bottom stone and falls into a wooden chute leading to the first floor where it is channeled into the bags.

Still able to grind corn, the Old Mill is one of the popular attractive exhibits of the Nantucket Historical Association.

OLD NORTH WHARF AND THE SOUTH TOWER

One of the three earliest wharves on the waterfront, Old North Wharf is the only one which now has a semblance of its nineteenth-century appearance. This view shows that section nearest Easy Street, with three summer homes and one of the old boathouses. Many whaleships cleared from Old North, and in the last century this wharf was the headquarters for packets running regularly between Nantucket and Baltimore, Norfolk and New Orleans. Upon its transition to the activities of a summer resort Old North featured the daily sailings of the large catboat *Dauntless*, bringing passengers around Brant Point to the bathing beach near the western jetty. A boat livery was also established here and in the days when pulling (row) boats were popular this was a favorite rendezvous for the old boatmen.

Further down the wharf is the famous Wharf Rat Club founded nearly fifty years ago in a ship chandlery, and still the gathering place for Islanders and summer residents who enjoy the opportunity of relaxing in an unusual setting.

High above the tree tops, the golden dome of the South Tower dominates the scene. Actually the second tower to be raised on the Unitarian Church on Orange Street, the well-proportioned edifice houses the town clock, with its four clock faces, with the bell above in the louvered section, and the lookout tower at the very top. Along with sounding the hours, the bell (which was cast in Lisbon, Portugal, in 1812) also strikes 52 times at 7 o'clock in the morning, at 12 noon, and at 9 o'clock in the evening. The custom in Nantucket is traditional—announcing the ancient times for going to work, taking lunch, and curfew.

WAUWINET—BEACH GRASS, SANDY SHORE
AND HARBOR

At the head of Nantucket's extensive inner harbor a narrow beach barrier
separates the calm waters from the surf of the open Atlantic and the area is
appropriately called the "Haulover," where the fishermen could haul their
dories from one shore to the other. Just to the south of this section is the little
settlement named Wauwinet, after the Indian sachem who once ruled over this
portion of the island. Charming in its shingled cottages and attractive hotel,
Wauwinet justly enjoys the protection of its private domain.

Between the Haulover and Wauwinet, the ocean beach rises just enough
to effectively bar the intrusion of the pounding surf into the quiet waters of the
upper harbor. The beach grass binds the sand into a natural bulwark, and in
varying degrees of height and width this sea beach extends in a curved forma-
tion to Great Point Lighthouse, some four miles away.

A little beach cottage accentuates the sweep of this grass-topped strand.
In the summer the golden, sandy strand, washed by the blue waters and
outlined by the curling surf is a welcomed haven for many bathers, sun-
worshippers, strollers and fishermen.

54

STARBUCK MANSIONS, THE "THREE BRICKS"

While not the first of the brick mansions built in the town, the three Starbuck houses on Main Street are the most widely known. These Georgian style dwellings were built in 1837–1838 by Joseph Starbuck, a prosperous whaling merchant, for his three sons, George, Matthew and William Starbuck, and are of identical architectural style.

Erected during a period when the island was approaching its nineteenth-century apex as a whaling port, the "three bricks," as they are popularly known, stand as proud reminders of the prosperity of the firm which Joseph Starbuck founded shortly after the War of 1812. From that time, when Nantucket made a remarkable recovery from the ravages of that ill-timed war, the Starbuck firm enjoyed a steady success, reflecting the sagacity and business acumen of its founder. Such whaleships as the *Hero, President*, and *Omega* brought home full cargoes and it was only natural that one of the fleet should be named the *Three Brothers*.

It was in the year 1835 that Joseph Starbuck purchased houses and land on Main Street where he had the three houses built. Skilled men, such as James Childs, carpenter, and Christopher Capen, mason, were the contractors and the first house was completed in 1837, followed closely by the others, all completed in 1838. Not only did Joseph finance the building but he retained ownership of the deeds until 1850, when they were transferred to the three sons, who by that time were full fledged members of the firm of Joseph Starbuck and Sons.

For years the houses were a centerpiece in the social affairs of this part of Main Street, called the "Court End." It was in one of Mrs. George Starbuck's front parlors, the West Brick, that the Nantucket Historical Association was organized in 1894. First to pass out of family ownership was the East Brick, but the Middle Brick is still in the possession of the descendants of Matthew Starbuck. All these fine homes are representatives of the sturdy qualities of a whaling merchant and his closely-knit family.

56

THE GREAT PONDS OF NANTUCKET

When the first settlers arrived they built their homesteads along the line of ponds that stretch across the width of the island. In forming a system of land ownership called the Proprietors of the Common and Undivided Lands of Nantucket, they controlled the ponds as well, and this ownership is still recognized.

One of these major ponds is called Hummock, and it extends from the North Head to the curving length that almost entirely surrounds a section called in the olden days "The Woods," but today is known as "Ram Pasture." As in all the island ponds the white and yellow perch are found and the wild ducks flock. That part of Hummock known as Clark's Cove is a favorite stopping place for the great geese as they pursue their migratory routes. Submerged aquatic plants as well as the emergent sedge and cattails thrive here.

The island ponds are important parts of the natural scene, providing areas for relaxation for many people. Scoured from the land by the glacier which formed the island as a terminal moraine, the ponds in the southern outwash plain were formed when the sea built sand barriers across their outlets. When the water level in these ponds becomes too high these sand barriers are cut through to allow the level to fall and thus permit an influx of salt water. But the salinity content is soon dissipated by natural conditions.

In recent years the Nantucket Conservation Foundation has been a strong factor in efforts to preserve these ponds, and this important organization deserves the support of all who love Nantucket.

58

THE 'SCONSET PUMP—VILLAGE CENTERPIECE

Situated on the bluff along the southeastern shore of Nantucket, the village of Siasconset, always called 'Sconset, has been a favored summer home for thousands. Well over a century ago it was a setting for the fishermen who built little huts in which they lived during the fishing seasons. Today these miniature cottages, and a number of replicas, are so much in demand that to obtain one it is often necessary to inherit it!

As a centerpiece for this unique village, the old 'Sconset Pump has served well over the years. The date of its first appearance is usually given as 1776, although many believe it is older as the fishermen were busy here a half century before that date. Although it no longer draws up water from the deep well, the Pump is still preserved by the Nantucket Historical Association as a symbol of the hardy people who first built this community, and the many who have sought to keep it unspoiled.

'Sconset needs no memorial or monument established to commemorate the past, to remind us that vigilant protection must be carried on, as long as it preserves the old 'Sconset Pump.

OLD 'SCONSET PUMP
THE WELL WAS DUG IN
-1776-

AULD LANG SYNE—'SCONSET'S OLDEST HOUSE

The little thoroughfare called Broadway (a name bestowed by the New York theatrical folk who adopted the village in the 1890s) has the largest grouping of old dwellings. On the west side of the street is the oldest of the little houses that range its length—a structure known for many years as Auld Lang Syne. Foreman, in his excellent study of the old houses of the village, describes it as the most ancient of the fishermen's huts, and built before 1700. A number of these tiny structures were moved from another fishing hamlet a few miles to the east with the interesting name of "Peedee."

Like other of the vintage dwellings at 'Sconset, Auld Lang Syne has many interesting architectural features, all of which are described in detail in Mr. Foreman's book as well as in Edward Underhill's earlier account of the village. Underhill left his impress on 'Sconset life. A visitor in the late 1870s he became a devotee and studied the old lore. In 1881 he began the construction of a number of cottages carefully designed in the style of the original homes of the fishermen. Today these replicas are often mistaken for the genuine structures.

Early in the nineteenth century many residents of the town fixed up the old houses of the village, and 'Sconset became a "summer place" for these townfolk. Among these were Captain Henry Coleman, a retired whaling master and clipper ship master, who added an extra room to Auld Lang Syne. In the last two decades of the century 'Sconset was "discovered" by the theatrical folk of New York. Many of the celebrities of the stage found a haven here, and their number was augmented by noted producers and directors. With the turn of the twentieth century 'Sconset was known as the "Actors' Colony."

From 1885 to 1917 a narrow-gauge railroad connected town and 'Sconset. This was the era before automobiles invaded the island and life in the village was of a nature that a contemporary account described as the "golden years." Margaret Fawcett Barnes has captured this period in her all too slender monograph "'Sconset Heyday."

TOWARD GREAT POINT, THE LONELY SENTINEL

The oldest lighthouse tower on Nantucket still stands on the end of Great Point, a tall lonely white sentinel, little changed from its building in 1818 when it replaced an earlier wooden structure. The keeper's lodge was destroyed by fire a few years ago and never replaced, as the Government operates the light by a remote control. Great Point, or Sandy Point as first named, may be approached from the sea or land. Like a curved finger it points towards Cape Cod's Monomoy Point, and the lighthouse has guarded mariners against becoming caught in the maze of shoals which dominate Nantucket Sound on the one hand and the rips off shore in the open Atlantic Ocean.

Great Point Rip has been a favorite fishing area as far back as can be recorded. Fighting bluefish and hungry bass, as well as cod and pollock may be caught from the cruisers "running the rip," or by rod and reel from the beach. Excursions for picnics, or just a day's outing attract the vacationer as well as the islander.

A Life Saving Station, later a U.S. Coast Guard installation, was located at Coskata, a mile and more from the lighthouse, but was closed after World War II and the buildings removed. During its years of service the Station took part in a number of notable rescues.

NANTUCKET HARBOR COMES ALIVE IN SUMMER

Nantucket's excellent harbor furnishes the visiting yachtsman with a wide anchorage area, should he prefer to anchor outside rather than enter the boat basin. The scene is always colorful and moving, with sleek schooners and sloops, ketches, yawls and motor sailers at their moorings. White sails flashing, outboards darting in and out, dinghys heading for shore and motor launches from the Yacht Club on their rounds, all comprise a busy summer seascape.

The green shore of Shimmo with its attractive homes adds a strong background to the scene, with the low sandy stretch of Coatue on the other hand. This island town affords a welcome landfall for the yachtsman when, after a cruise across the Sound, he sights the north shore and heads for the bell buoy and the jetties' mouth, slipping at last into the channel leading to Brant Point and the inner harbor.

Where once the whaleships tugged at their anchors and the town served as a home for mariners familiar with all the great oceans, today the yachtsman finds a welcome haven.

66

A REWARDING RESTORATION—THE JOSEPH GARDNER HOUSE

If there is a certain kind of pleasure for those who appreciate the charming qualities of an old house, it is probably best enjoyed by those who have restored one. The Joseph Gardner House at 139 Main Street was built before 1790, but had been converted into a carriage barn in the early 1800s by George C. Gardner, who built the large white mansion next door. In 1928 Miss Gladys Wood bought the carriage barn and had it moved some 500 feet to its present location. Alfred Shurrocks, an architect, carefully supervised the restoration, and the result is one of the most outstanding of the early period houses in the town. Constructed with four bays, three of which determine the size of the keeping room, the framing has two great summer, or supporting beams, running from front to rear, with the smaller floor joists fitted. The first-story corner posts have bracketed tops, which are of the gun-stop design on the second floor. A side ell and a lean-to addition on the back are natural developments. The small-paned sash in the casement windows completes the seventeenth-century appearance of this thoroughly satisfying restoration.

The Gardner house is typical of the earliest island dwellings. Small but strongly constructed, the sills resting on the ground, with wide fireplaces, shingled side walls and roof, these little houses were family headquarters, a haven from the winter's chill and a gathering place for the relatives. Wood for the building of these island dwellings came by sloop from New Hampshire and Maine, as there was no dimensional timber on the island of native growth. The frugal settlers guarded their homes carefully, and it is not strange to find many houses moved across the island to the new town at the Great Harbor, thus becoming older than the streets which became their new location.

68

THE OPEN-AIR MARKETS ON MAIN STREET'S SQUARE

A colorful activity on busy Main Street's Square each summer is the open-air market. Farmers bring both vegetables and flowers from their gardens and, after backing their trucks to the sidewalk curbs, conduct their sales directly to the people. The scene is always informal, with on-lookers vying with customers for a vantage place. The movement and touch of color is a welcome addition to the Square.

Such a custom is traditional on Nantucket. Each spring and fall, when the codfish are running, fishermen bring them freshly caught and sell them on the street. One of the practices no longer a part of Main Street was the auction, with two marts on the lower Square offering commodities ranging from fresh meat to household furniture. Whenever the town crier made his rounds a full notice of these auctions was always given full voice.

In the background may be seen the sign over the entrance to the "Hub," at the corner of Federal and Main streets, where the daily newspapers are sold and periodicals are available. This in itself is of interest, especially on Sundays, when the populace lines up and the "queue," as the British call it, extends for several hundred feet down Federal Street during the time the papers are being dispensed.

70

LITTLE LANES LEAD TO PEACEFUL VISTAS

The sojourner may often come upon a narrow lane leading from one of the streets and not connecting with any other thoroughfare. These are usually entrances to private property and, while not generally traveled by the public, do afford unusual glimpses and vistas. One of these is the lane extending north from Upper Main Street, with a double branching at the end—one way leading to Quarter Mile Hill and the other becoming the entrance to another private estate.

This latter by-way, with its scallop-shell drive, leads to where an old house sits overlooking an expanse of meadow. The house originally stood on Main Street but a quarter century ago was carefully moved to its present site. Of a double lean-to style, with a ridge chimney, and shed roof on the west side, it has been only slightly altered and still faces the south.

Richard Gardner and his family owned the land north of Main Street, west of Gardner, east of New Lane, and south of North Liberty Street. The area was known as the "Crooked Record" because its perimeter on the land map was so irregular. Several lanes led into this extensive area and those still existing are the entrances to private estates.

72

EAST ROOM OF THE JETHRO COFFIN HOUSE

When a visitor who has come to the island for the first time approaches the Oldest House on Nantucket he immediately senses the historic significance of this ancient structure. Built in 1686 for Jethro Coffin and his bride, Mary Gardner, the time-honored story reveals that the breach between the Coffins and Gardners was finally bridged by the union of Tristram's grandson, Jethro, and John Gardner's daughter Mary; and that the land was donated by the Gardners and the timber for the house by the Coffins.

Until the late 1860s the house had been occupied by the Coffin, Paddack and Turner families, then abandoned, and but for the interest of a Coffin descendant from Poughkeepsie, New York, who purchased it in 1881, it might have literally collapsed. Four decades later the house was deeded to the Nantucket Historical Association and restoration was immediately commenced. Architectural historians are in disagreement as to the completed work, but local historians are content to have this ancient structure intact once more.

Annually visited by thousands of visitors, the Oldest House provides a rare glimpse into the way the seventeenth-century islanders lived and worked. Furnished with period pieces as closely as possible, the rooms on the first and second floors are all accessible. The east room, or dining room, has the largest of the huge fireplaces and, as the photograph shows, is a pleasant and light-filled room.

With its long north roof sloping to the rear, its casement windows and sturdy side walls, the Oldest House conveys that feeling for the past which brings to it the very atmosphere of the earlier times. The great center chimney, with its projection of bricks on the front face shaped like a horseshoe, gives the name "Horse-Shoe House," by which it was once commonly known. However, as the horseshoe in this case is inverted and hardly the accepted symbol of good luck, one qualified observer noted the design might have been intended to depict a wish-bone!

74

WILLIAM HADWEN HOUSES—THE GREEK REVIVAL

Directly opposite the three brick Starbuck houses on cobbled Main Street are two imposing, white-pillared mansions that were built in the years 1844–1845 by a whaling merchant named William Hadwen. Their tall columns, wide porticoes and dignified proportions are in the best tradition of the Greek Revival period of American architecture, and their construction marked the high point of Nantucket's nineteenth-century whaling prosperity.

William Hadwen came to Nantucket in 1820 to carry on his business as a silversmith. He married Eunice Starbuck, one of the daughters of Joseph Starbuck, soon became an investor in whaleships and a few years later formed a company with his brother-in-law Nathaniel Barney, who had married Eliza Starbuck, another of Joseph Starbuck's daughters. The firm of Hadwen & Barney prospered and among the ships in which they owned a majority of shares were the *Alpha* and *Enterprise*.

The Hadwens were not blessed with children and they virtually adopted a niece, Amelia Swain, who lived just down the street. In 1845 William had 94 Main Street built for this niece, directly next door to his own mansion, into which she moved soon after her marriage to George Wright. It then became known as the Wright Mansion. The couple lived here for only a comparatively few years when they moved to San Francisco, and George Wright became the first of the Californian congressmen elected to the Congress in Washington.

The architect and builder of these two handsome mansions, Frederick Brown Coleman, an island contractor, adapted his plans from the fabled Temple of the Winds. Large, high-ceilinged rooms, well-proportioned rooms, elaborate mantle pieces, tall windows and ornate furnishings were quite a departure from the traditional Nantucket style of architecture and living. The Hadwens were civic minded and their home became an active center for community enterprises. The Wright mansion passed from that family's hands in the 1880s and has been owned by several people, the present owners having done much to restore its handsome original.

A decade ago the Hadwen House, at the corner of Pleasant and Main streets, was presented to the Nantucket Historical Association by the daughter of Mr. and Mrs. Joseph Satler, the last occupants of the mansion. Now known as the Hadwen-Satler Memorial, it is open to the public daily during the season and over the winter holidays and the group of hostesses tell the story of the mansion and its furnishings.

MARIA MITCHELL'S BIRTHPLACE

The birthplace of Maria Mitchell on Vestal Street has been carefully restored by the association formed in 1902 which bears her name. It was first opened to the public in 1904, with Mrs. Mary Mitchell Albertson, a daughter of Peleg Mitchell, as the first Curator. Mrs. Albertson, a cousin of Maria Mitchell, had been born in the house. William Mitchell, the Quaker father of Maria Mitchell, had purchased the house from Simeon Gardner early in 1818, and on August 1 of that year daughter Maria was born here. It is a house of quiet charm, two and a half stories in height, with the rooms comfortably homey, the windows large and well spaced, a great central chimney, and a walk on the roof. The William Mitchells lived here until 1837, when they moved to an apartment over the Pacific Bank's business rooms. Maria's early instruction in astronomy took place in the Vestal Street house.

Hezekiah Swain was the builder of 1 Vestal Street, and Simeon Gardner lived here until William Mitchell bought the house. Peleg Mitchell, who followed his brother as the owner, built the ell on the northwest corner, now the kitchen.

The room depicted in the photograph conveys the restful atmosphere of the Quaker household. Something of the close association of father and daughter pervades these rooms, with just enough of the austerity of their lives to help in understanding that search for knowledge which characterized both their lives.

78

WHEN THE DAILY STEAMBOATS DEPART

Again, the observation tower of the North Church presents an excellent opportunity to capture a typical summer scene along the waterfront. The beach in the foreground is called the "Children's Beach," having been set aside forty years ago by the town as a protected area for youngsters. At their moorings in the inner harbor's basin, between Brant Point and Steamboat Wharf, a cluster of small craft may be seen, their number including catboats, rainbows and launches. The U.S. Coast Guard headquarters on Brant Point occupies a good section of the land, with the lookout towers, signal masts, boathouse, and other structures in a complex. The old lighthouse tower built in 1856, without its lens assembly on top, may be clearly seen, although the present little lighthouse at the Point's end is obscured.

Rounding the Point is the handsome steamer *Nantucket*, built nearly two decades ago, which, after some problems of a mechanical nature, has become a dependable link in the marine transportation maintained by the Steamship Authority. As the most commodious passenger vessel in the fleet, it is hoped that the *Nantucket* may continue to make her daily trips to and from Woods Hole for many years to come.

GIFT SHOPS HAVE BECOME NUMEROUS

It may be said that during the years since the end of World War II the town has become literally sprinkled with gift shops. Offering a wide variety of wares, these places find a steady procession of customers, and the fact that they re-open with each season indicates their success is as constant as their regular appearances.

As hardy perennials in the bouquet of shops are those places which handle antiques. The photograph shows one of these attractive stores, a small but well-equipped shop, with a rose vine lending its own appeal to the setting. Those who frequent the out-of-way as well as the established places enjoy "just looking," with more than an occasional "bargain" to lend excitement to the day.

Nantucket town is an ideal place for the shopper, with all but a few shops within walking distance of the center. An automobile may be dispensed with while shopping at the gift shops, or may be left at a distance from busy Main Street Square. A visit to the smaller antique store affords an introduction to visits at the larger places, where amazing amounts of attractive material may be found. The seeker in the market of antiques has his own particular satisfaction in finding and buying that article which has its own especial appeal.

82

ALONG GARDNER STREET

Gradually ascending the slope from North Liberty Street, the length of Gardner Street leads to Main Street's Monument Square. Originally called Queen Street it was later changed to Gardner, a more logical name as that family owned practically all the land to the west.

The view is from the porch of the Captain Robert Joy house, looking south. In the foreground is the fence fronting the Edward Folger house; and on the left is a typical Nantucket dwelling, with its four-bayed front, shingled side walls, transom over the door and a center chimney. The large dwelling next door, with the two chimneys, originally stood on Ray's Court, off Main Street, and was moved to this location in 1831. It was at one time the home of Captain William Cartwright, a clipper ship master who was lost at sea in 1864 when his ship, the famous *Houqua*, disappeared somewhere in the Pacific Ocean without a trace.

Although a short street compared to North Liberty, Gardner Street has an interesting variety of dwellings ranging in age from the ancient home of Christopher Starbuck (1690–1720) to Captain Joy's Greek Revival style mansion, and the variety of its doorway designs is noteworthy.

84

BOAT BASINS, HAVEN FOR YACHTSMEN

The most significant changes along the waterfront have been the installation of a series of boat basins. These areas are within the confines of three wharves, which in themselves have had major restoration and renovation. A wooden breakwater guards the entrances to the boat basins. At the peak of a summer season these mooring places are filled to capacity. An amazing variety of marine craft may be observed, sleek cabin cruisers, large motor vessels, sailing sloops, ketches and schooners.

There is always activity along the wharves, with the shops and the artists' studios attracting their patrons, and the occupants of the waterfront cottages entertaining guests or enjoying the moving scene.

But the art of rowing has not been entirely neglected, as pulling boats, large and small, are to be found throughout the docks, with an occasional modern dinghy being maneuvered to and fro.

86

THE PACIFIC CLUB

The large brick structure at the lower end of Main Street's Square has been known as the Pacific Club since 1854 when a group of Nantucket shipmasters formed the Club. Before that time it was owned by the Commercial Insurance Company. Built by William Rotch, the outstanding Quaker whaling merchant in New England, it was the Rotch Counting House and the firm's headquarters in the last decades of the eighteenth century. From the structure cleared the *Beaver* and *Dartmouth*, loaded with whale oil for London, and on return voyages they brought cargoes of the "detestable tea" which caused the Boston Tea Party. In 1783, the ship *Bedford* took her manifest from this Rotch Counting House for a full cargo of whale oil to England, and sailing up the Thames hoisted the first American flag ever flown before the port of London—and this before the Treaty of Paris was signed.

When the U.S. Customs was established in 1789 the Rotch building became the first Nantucket Custom House, continuing until 1913 when it was abandoned by the government. The Weather Bureau began its station here in 1886, and the first telegraph cable to Nantucket was connected to its office. In 1916 Joseph Brock, President of the Pacific, inaugurated the island's first telephone service by calling from the Captain's Room to his friend William Macy in Medford a few minutes after the service was officially opened with a ceremony at the Nantucket Atheneum.

In the foreground is the old iron drinking fountain for horses, which was first placed on Upper Main Street in 1881 but early in this century was moved to its present location in the lower Square. This part of the cobbled street is now called Max Wagner Square in honor of Lieut. Wagner, who was killed during the American involvement in the Philippines in 1899. The old fountain is not a relic of a distant past. It was an important part of the street, for the horse and wagon were not supplanted by the automobile until 1918, when the "horseless carriage" was finally allowed legally to drive through the town.

88

"THE COMMONS," RICH HUES OF AUTUMN

When the fall season sweeps across the island the open heathland becomes a magic carpet of color. This moorland has a variety of plant-life—bayberry bushes, sweet fern, huckleberry, trailing arbutus, pasture rose, bearberry, golden aster and grasses. Rutted roads traverse these stretches, leading over the undulating terrain to low hills, to fragrant valleys and tiny, hidden ponds.

Across the center of the island, between the Polpis and 'Sconset roads, one finds the full range of this varied landscape, with the borders of Gibbs Pond offering delightful places for a pause. Thickets of scrub oak serve as cover for rabbits and pheasant, while an occasional deer may emerge from the pine groves. The swamps are thick with wild grape vines, Virginia creeper, sweet pepper bush and high-bush blueberry, and in the deeper recesses are stands of beech trees and maples that grow as high as the hilltops that protect but then are controlled by the wind. Poison ivy must be watched for as in some places it is rampant.

There are two factors that the nature lovers of Nantucket are constantly concerned with, the beach-buggies and jeeps that thoughtless drivers steer over the open heath and along the beaches, and the increase in the scrub pine which threatens to overcome some of the old pasture land.

The open heathland of Nantucket has been called "The Commons" from the time the first settlers drew up plans for the use of the undivided land as a common pasture land for their sheep and cattle. With the important and vital acquisition of portions of this old terrain by the Nantucket Conservation Foundation, and similar control by other agencies, it may be possible some day to apply this ancient and meaningful name once again to these priceless areas of the island.

THE CHANGING SCENE "OUT OF TOWN"

The natural attractions of Nantucket have become so much a part of its economy that the loss of any part of one of them has a detrimental effect upon the whole. These physical assets range from the atmosphere of the historic town, its accommodations for visitors, and its services; the opportunities for swimming, cycling, golfing and other recreational activities; to the open expanses of beach and heathland, and moors stretching out to the sea.

Whenever some of these open areas are converted into modern housing developments there is a sobering aftermath—a time for serious reflection on what effect this will have on the future of the island.

As the photograph shows some of the recent construction in these "out of town" areas has brought about a marked change in the old, familiar scenes.

92

REFLECTIONS IN A BOAT BASIN

One of the first of the modern boat basins along the waterfront was installed between Straight and Old South wharves—two of the earliest constructed at Sherborn—old Nantucket.

As the present-day cruisers, sloops and sports-fishermen lie safe at their berths, the quiet morning water surface reflects the hulls and piles, with only a slight rippling in the mirror of the tidal flow.

A century ago the last Nantucket whaleship, the bark *Oak* cast off her lines from Straight Wharf and slipped out of the harbor, never to return. Aside from a brief effort to establish a fishing fleet here, the only large craft to frequent the wharves were the packet schooners, coal schooners, quahaug draggers and catboats.

Today, the island's wealth from the sea is in her shellfish fleet which uses these docks, the sports fishing boats and the visiting yachtsmen. During the season Nantucket's new boat basins provide all the necessary services for hundreds of visiting yachts, and those who thoughtfully send ahead for reservations find the accommodations are equal and often superior to those found anywhere on the coast.

94